UNKISSED MEMORY

"I love, am loved, yet starve here,

in this hollow, barren land,

Neither lover nor beloved...

just a suffering, shattered man."

—from The Twin Shores of Absence

UNKISSED MEMORY

(Poems on Loving Someone You Can't Have)

-By Ramcharan Vemulapudi

UNKISSED MEMORY

A Year of Silent Love

Publisher: Ramcharan Vemulapudi

Publisher Contact: ramcharan24dd@gmail.com

ISBN: 978-93-343-9829-8

First Edition: September 2025

For the one who inspired a universe

within the quiet confines of a single heart—

though you will never know it was yours.

Table of Contents

- A collection of prose-style poems and reflections, capturing fleeting moments of a silent love.
- This section will contain a series of short, impactful reflections

Prologue: The Genesis of a Ghost

This is not a love story. It is the blueprint of an absence. The ghost of a heartbeat. It is the detailed cartography of a territory that was never explored, yet is known to me with the intimate precision of a lonely god who created a world only to never set foot upon its soil. This is the chronicle of a year spent in the silent, sacred worship of a stranger—a year where the most real and defining relationship of my life was one that existed entirely within the confines of my own skull.

We live in a world that only validates love when it is witnessed. It requires the grammar of interaction: the spoken word, the returned gaze, the tangible proof of a hand held, a promise made, a kiss given. We are taught that love is a transaction, a dialogue, a shared narrative. But what of the love that is a monologue? The love that is a sovereign, solitary nation with a population of one? What language does it speak? It speaks in poetry. It speaks in the silent, screaming verses that follow you down crowded streets and into the quiet desperation of your room. It is a soundless orchestra performing a symphony for an audience of shadows, and for one entire year, I was its composer, its conductor, and its only prisoner.

It began, as these things often do, not with a bang but with a whisper of light. A glance that lasted a fraction of a second longer than propriety dictated. In that fleeting moment, something tectonic shifted in the unexplored depths of my being. It was not her beauty alone, though that was undeniable; it was the unsettling, immediate certainty that I was in the presence of a walking sonnet. She moved through the world as a finished work of art, a living elegy to some greater beauty the rest of us had forgotten. And I, a mere spectator, felt the terrifying urge to become a scholar of her existence. This was the dawning, the genesis of my silent obsession. The poems in the first section of this book—Springtime Love, Lost in Her, Her—are not exaggerations. They are forensic documents. They are the minutes from the first meeting of a heart that had just discovered its purpose: to admire, to yearn, to document this sublime discovery.

What follows a dawning but an inferno? The initial awe curdled into a sweet, all-consuming sickness. This was no longer mere admiration; it was a possession of the spirit. I became a addict in need of a fix, and my drug was the sight of her. A five-second glimpse could fuel my imagination for days. My mind became a loom, weaving intricate tapestries of conversation we would never have, of moments that would never occur. I constructed a entire personality from the tilt of her head, the sound of her laughter from across a room—a sound I desperately tried to isolate from the noise of the world and claim as my own. This was the season of Eternal Devotion, of Wildfire and Ash. I was the miner in Fool's Hope, endlessly tunneling through the rock of my own longing, knowing the treasure was never meant for my hands, yet incapable of stopping the dig. The love burned with the intensity of a star, but like a star, it was distant, untouchable, and its light was that of a dead thing, already gone by the time it reached me.

And then, as it must, the doubt began to seep in. The monsoon to my personal summer. The high fever of infatuation broke, leaving behind the damp chill of reality. The mind, so adept at building castles in the air, eventually remembers the law of gravity. This was the slow, v melancholic turning. The questions began to pierce the daydreams. Who was I, really, to her? A ghost. A blur in the periphery. A face in a crowd she passed through without seeing. The fear articulated in The Fear of Losing You became a self-fulfilling prophecy—how can you lose what you never had? You lose the dream of it. You lose the potential. And that loss is somehow more profound, for it mourns a future that had a thousand beautiful possibilities, now narrowed down to the one, bleak reality of silence.

This fear gave birth to a profound loneliness, a winter of the soul. The poems from this period—Dear…, A Vault for Sorrows, Caged Bird—are the cries in that winter. They are the sound of a heart realizing it has been speaking into a void for months. The love, once a source of radiant energy, now became a cage. I was the bird singing a song for someone who not only couldn't hear it, but didn't know the song existed. The Mirage of Love faded, and I was left standing in the barren desert of my own choices, parched and alone. The agony of The Twin Shores of Absence is the unique torture of the one-sided lover: to be simultaneously heartbroken over the one you cannot have and consumed with guilt over the one you cannot love in return. It is a double helix of despair.

But a soul cannot winter forever. Slowly, almost imperceptibly, a new understanding began to form. This was not spring again, not a cyclical return to the beginning. That would be too simple, too naive. This was something else entirely. This was the Holy Gray. It was the realization that this entire journey, for all its pain, had not been a waste. It had been the most intense and creative period of my life. The silence had not starved me; it had forced me to feed myself from my own internal resources. I had learned the intricate geography of my own heart through the act of mapping it onto her. The poems I write with secrets only storms know and Windows of the Void are born from this place. They are the artifacts of a soul that has stared into the abyss of its own making and found not nothingness, but a strange, new depth.

The love did not disappear; it transmuted. It was no longer a desperate ache for reciprocity. It became, as expressed in the final poem, I know..., a pure, self-contained act of giving. "The greatest love asks nothing in return from you." I learned to love the love itself, not its object. I learned to cherish the beauty of the feeling, even if the cause of the feeling would never know of its existence. The unkissed memory became sacred precisely because it was unkissed. It remained perfect, uncorrupted by the messy realities of human interaction. It was my Sistine Chapel ceiling—a masterpiece painted on the walls of my own solitude, never meant to be seen by its muse.

This book, then, is that chapel. These poems are the frescoes. They are my confessions, my devotions, my screams into a pillow, and my whispered prayers to a god I wasn't sure was listening. They are the bridge I built from my longing, which you now cross, seeing every nail and plank that went into its construction—the heartwood of hope, the mortar of despair.

You hold in your hands the anatomy of a silence. It is the story of how I loved a girl and found a realer version of myself in the process. How I learned that the most profound conversations are often the ones we have with ourselves, and that the most enduring love affairs are sometimes the ones we never have with anyone else.

This is not a love story. It is something more complex, more fragile, and in its own way, more beautiful. It is the story of an unkissed memory. And it is my story. Turn the page, and listen to the echo.

About the Author and This Book

This book was not written by an author. It was excavated by a boy who felt too much and said too little.

If you're reading this, you've already stepped into the most private space of my mind. These pages are not a performance; they are a crime scene. They are the evidence of a year-long heartbreak I inflicted entirely upon myself, and this is my statement.

I am, by every definition, an introvert. Crowds don't energize me; they drain me. Small talk feels like a foreign language I've never mastered. My world has always been internal, a landscape of thought and feeling that I rarely, if ever, grant anyone a visa to visit. For me, connection was never found in loud rooms or groups of friends. It was found in the quiet observation of a single, captivating person. And that's where this story begins.

She was from my college. I won't use her name here, because to me, she was never just a name. She was a collection of details, a living work of art I studied from a distance. The specific way her hair fell across her shoulders, the sound of her laugh—a sound I'd try to catch from across the class like it was a secret frequency only my heart could tune into. She was my muse in the most terrifyingly real sense. She existed in the world, tangible and real, and I existed in the shadow she cast.

I loved her. I loved her with the kind of all-consuming, desperate intensity that only an introvert's heart can manufacture. It's a love that has no outlet, no release valve. Because I never, not once, told her a single word. How could I? What would I even say. The gap between the grandeur of what I felt and the awkwardness of my reality was a canyon I could never cross. My voice would catch in my throat. My hands would sweat. My carefully rehearsed sentences would shatter into incoherent dust the moment any opportunity, however small, presented itself. So, I chose silence. I chose the safety of my own imagination over the terrifying gamble of rejection.

And so, I built a world where we were together. In my mind, we had a thousand conversations. I made her laugh. comforted her when she was sad. I told her all the things I was writing down in these poems. She was the silent star of every single story I ever told myself to get through the day. This book, from Springtime Love to The Unkissed Memory, is that world. It's the detailed transcript of a relationship that was, for all intents and purposes, a beautifully constructed fiction.

The poems in The Dawning section are from that first, breathless stage. They are wide-eyed and full of a wonder that feels almost naive to me now. I saw her as an angel, a goddess, a springtime miracle. I was the cuckoo bird singing for a reason only I understood. I was lost in her, and the thought of being found was terrifying. You Are... and A Distant Lighthouse weren't metaphors I crafted; they were literal, desperate truths. She was the lighthouse, and I was perpetually the ship adrift, forever watching the light but never making it to shore.

The Inferno is where that admiration curdled into a painful, beautiful agony. It was no longer just a crush; it was a possession. The poem Captivated isn't an exaggeration—it's a clinical diagnosis. I was a prisoner of my own devotion. Eternal Devotion is the peak of this madness, a poem where I literally deconstruct myself to build a monument to her. It's unsettling to read now, but it's honest. That's how it felt. I would have burned myself to ash for just a moment of her attention. Wildfire and Ash is the perfect title for that feeling—I was both the destructive fire and the lonely aftermath.

Then came the slow, painful realization that forms The Fading. This is where the cracks in my fantasy began to show. The poem The Fear of Losing You is based on a real, haunting conversation I had with myself. I was so terrified that if by some miracle I got her attention, I would inevitably be myself—awkward, quiet, unremarkable—and she would lose interest. So, I pre-emptively accepted the loss. I decided I was not worthy. It was a self- fulfilling prophecy of despair. She is gold, I'm just the miner became my mantra. I was the one digging in the dirt, and she was the priceless treasure I could never own. I saw myself as fundamentally lesser, a background character in her story. This wasn't her doing; it was mine. It was the story I told myself to make the silence make sense.

The Hollowing is the consequence of that story. This is the darkest section of the book because it was the darkest part of my year. The poems Dear… and A Vault for Sorrows are the cries of someone who has poured all of their emotional capacity into a void. I felt like a hollow shell, a container for a love that had nowhere to go. The profound loneliness of Loneliness held me softly is real. It's not a poetic turn of phrase; it's a description of a state of being. Loneliness became my only companion, and it held me because no one else did. The Twin Shores of Absence is the brutal math of my situation: I was stranded between the person I couldn't have and the person I couldn't be for anyone else.

I ended up in The Echo not through some triumphant overcoming of my nature, but through sheer exhaustion. I had felt everything there was to feel. I had run the entire emotional marathon and collapsed at the finish line. The poems here, like I know… and Holy Gray, are not victories. They are surrenders. They are the quiet, tired understanding that some loves are not meant to be spoken. They are meant to be felt, endured, and transformed into something else. I learned that love doesn't always need a target to be real. The feeling itself was real. The ache was real. The art it created is real.

So, why publish this? Why put this intensely private, often embarrassing confession out into the world?

Because I know I'm not the only one.

I know there is someone else out there who lives more in their head than in the world. Someone who has loved from a

distance, who has crafted entire futures with someone who doesn't know their name. This book is for you. You are not alone in your silence. Your quiet love is not less valid than the loud, proclaimed ones. It is, in its own way, more pure. It asks for nothing in return.

This book is my way of finally telling the story. Not to her— she will likely never read this, and that's okay. This was never really about her. It was always about me. It was about the boy who watched, who dreamed, who hurt, and who, ultimately, wrote his way out of the silence.

This book is my one and only word to her. The only one I could ever manage.

Thank you for reading

—A boy who loved quietly

PART I: THE DAWNING

A Heart Unmoored

Springtime Love

She is the spring, the crown of every season,

I'm the cuckoo bird who sings for good reason.

She is the spring, the queen of renewal,

My heart awakens, bathed in love's warm hue.

She is the spring, the time of blooming,

In her warmth, my heart begins to blossom.

She is the spring, with a touch so warming,

My heart's snow melts, love transforming.

She is the spring, bringing forth new beginnings,

Hope and delight, in her light, winnings.

Lost in Her

My soul tangled in her curls,

My eyes drown in her gaze.

Her beauty floods my thoughts,

Her breath makes my skin blaze.

Heart, once mine, now hers to keep—

Love has found where heart waits,

And opens up the golden gates.

Her

In realms where language fails to capture grace,

She moves, a living poem, through time and space.

With every breath, a verse so softly sighed,

In every glance, a melody implied.

Her presence is a sonnet, pure and bright,

A luminous beacon in the dark of night.

Her gaze, a verse no words could ever speak,

A rhythm where the shadows softly meet.

Her hair, a flowing epic, dark and deep,

Where secrets of the universe did sleep.

Her smile, a spark, igniting joy within,

A moment's grace where new worlds could begin.

Her voice, a balm, a comfort to the soul,

That made the broken spirit whole.

Her touch, a lyric, gentle as the rain,

A sweet refrain that eased all earthly pain.

Her spirit danced beyond all earthly art,

A masterpiece no human hand could chart.

A Garden for Your Beauty

Your presence
lights my face aglow,
like the moon
in the sun's warm flow.

My heart, a garden,
where your beauty blooms,
a masterpiece of love,
dispelling all my gloom.

Your gentle touch
lifts my spirit high,
like a kite that dances
in the open sky.

Thoughts of you
make love wildly start,
leaving me breathless,
with a full heart.

You Are...

In the whisper of the breeze,
your name I hear;
in the calm of the night,
your presence is near.

You are the moon,
glowing in every phase;
I am the child,
lost within your gaze.

You are the night sky
where my soul flies,
like the aurora
shining in your eyes.

You are the sunrise after
every long night;
I'm the sleepless night,
dreaming of your light.

You are the dawn,
painting my world bright;
I'm the shadow,
shrinking with your light.

You are the ocean,
deep and wide;
I am the tide,
forever by your side.

You are the song
a melody divine;
I am the verse
where your love aligns.

You are the dream,
the wish upon a star;
I am the believer,
knowing you are never far.

A Distant Lighthouse

A heart's voyage, through shadows,

I am the ship, adrift and lost.

You are a lighthouse I cannot touch,

A beacon of light, a source of despair.

The Silent Orchestra

In the quiet where words find no release,

a silent orchestra begins to piece.

A score of feelings, soft and low,

a rhythm only two hearts know.

Unseen, unheard by outer ear,

but in the soul, it rings so clear.

PART II: THE INFERNO

Adoration and Agony

Captivated

The room shrinks to her, a single point
where thought unravels, motion stills.
I wear a mask of stone,
though inside, my heart's a wild thing
that beats against its cage.

I am a branch in a storm,
bending toward her gravity.
Each time I try to turn away,
I'm pulled back to her light.

I pray for a slow escape—
a single feather,
dropped and free.

The Unkissed Memory

Under the gentle moonlight, your lips open like a red rose, revealing hidden truths and filling the silence with a powerful song.

Your lips, both soft and intense, stir up deep feelings within me, like a moth drawn to a light that hasn't even been lit yet.

My breath catches whenever you speak. Nothing tastes as sweet as your kiss, which sets the air on fire. Every curve of your lips, every sigh, makes my heart race with desire.

Others can look for grand adventures, but I'll stay in this moment, where every star seems to have been traded for this experience.

Because when you kiss me, the entire universe shrinks to just us, a perfect,

intense feeling. Even if the world fell apart, I'd only want to explore the map of your lips.

So take me, enchantress. Let your passionate kiss wash away everything I've ever known. No one could stop this. losing myself in you is true freedom.

Eternal Devotion

If I were to create your form, so perfectly divine,
I would willingly offer this body of mine.
I'd burn it to ash, a sacrifice of self,
Using the remnants as clay upon a shelf,
To mold your likeness with unwavering devotion,
A testament to a love beyond all motion.

My own blood, a vibrant, crimson hue,
Would serve as the paint, faithful and true,
With which I would colour your form with tender care,
Tracing each line, each curve, beyond compare.

And my very bones,
I would crush to fine dust,
Mixing them with the blood, in sacred trust,
To create a bindi, a mark upon your brow,
A symbol of my devotion, a sacred vow.

From the delicate pathways of my veins,

I'd weave a crown of intricate beauty, I believe,
Fit for my queen, a goddess in my sight,
Adorned with the essence of my heart's own light.

And this very heart, I would shatter into pieces small,
Transforming them into ornaments, to grace you all,
Each fragment a jewel, reflecting my deep love,
A treasure beyond all measure, sent from above.

My muscles, strong and resilient, I would then reshape,
Into floral masterpieces, an intricate escape,
Each petal a testament to the beauty I see,
A garden of devotion, blooming eternally.

And even my skin, I would peel away with grace,
To fashion a garment, to clothe you in this space,
A covering of love, a shield against all harm,
Protecting you always, keeping you forever warm.

Like a devotee kneeling before a sacred shrine,
Lost in reverence, in a love truly divine,

You are my goddess, the object of my deepest desire,

Eternally mine, fueling my heart's fire.

You are the essence of my every thought,

A vision of perfection, divinely brought.

No Lexicon

No lexicon could hold her essence true,

No painted canvas capture all her hue.

Wildfire and Ash

Your blaze turns my heart to wildfire,

Your name, a new kind of weather.

Your words are sparks in dusk's dim breath,

I'm the air pulled in by your quiet heat.

You rise like a story told in flame,

I'm ash learning how to fly again.

No science or myth—just light, just air:

Your flame writes the sky… and I burn there.

The Agony of Liberation

I stabbed myself in the heart

with the knife called love.

My body writhes,

bleeding my soul into the air.

But my soul rises from the wound,

a creature of light,

its wings now free from its cage of bone.

My Angel of Unrest

She is an angel in my sight,
A vision pure, my heart's delight.
If chance allowed, I'd kneel and pray,
To worship her in every way.

Butterflies dance within my core,
A thrill that kills, yet leaves me more—
Excitement, joy, a sweet unrest,
Her presence stirs my soul's deep quest.

Her cheeks, a haven soft and near,
Where my lips long to linger here.
Her voice, a melody divine,
Trapped in my ears, a heavenly sign.

Her smile, like the crescent moon so fair,
Illuminates my dark despair,
A gentle glow, a guiding beam,
Filling my night with love's sweet dream.

Unreachable

Unreachable, they taunt and tease,

These silent longings that give no peace.

I yearn for them with every breath,

As sleep evades, a phantom death.

PART III: THE FADING

First Cracks in the Sanctuary

The Silent Verse

I am a poem, forever misunderstood,
A cryptic script, a shadow in the wood.
A withered plant, forgotten, left to die,
A grounded bird, longing for the sky.

Yet you, alone, hold the mystic key,
Deciphering my verses, setting my spirit free.
You light the darkness, vast and deep,
Lifting me high, from where shadows sleep.

You are the gardener, tending to my soul,
The gentle hand that makes me whole.
A whispering breeze, lifting me high,
From shadowed ground to open sky.

Hidden Depths

Eyes, like peaceful lakes, seem calm and bright,

But deep inside, feelings hide from sight.

A secret storm, wild and deep,

Emotions hidden, in shadows they creep.

Oceans, like beautiful eyes, vast and calm above,

But below, chaos and a mighty shove.

Strong currents swirl unseen,

Mysteries lie, in depths serene.

Both have secrets, things we don't see,

A quiet way of talking, silently.

Beneath the calm, stories hide,

Truths concealed, in the quiet tide.

The Fear of Losing You

She turned to me, eyes searching, and asked, "Why don't you talk to me every day? You are the only thing that makes me happy, makes me feel so free. You are the only one I like to spend my whole time with." I met her gaze, the familiar ache tightening in my chest.

"Whatever we like," I began, my voice low, "if we see it, do it, eat it, or hear it every day, slowly, slowly we start to dislike it."

Her reply was swift, almost defiant. "But I don't get bored like that."

Her words unraveled something in me. A wave of raw, painful honesty surged up, bypassing my usual restraint. "You can say that,"

I countered, the words sharp, "you can say you never get bored of the things you like, no matter how many times you do them, see them, eat them, or hear them.

But you don't want to admit that you've lost interest in them, which is why you still pretend to like them." Silence hung

heavy for a moment before

I laid bare the true source of my distance, the fear I carried like a stone. "That's why I don't talk to you every day, even though it's so hard for me. Deep down, I always want to spend every second with you.

But I know... I know one day you'll leave me when you lost interest in me."

The Untouched Shore

My heart is like a big, blue ocean,

Always looking towards you with devotion.

I keep sending waves, trying to reach your calm shore,

But your shores remain untouched.

I understand at last, the distance we hold.

So my waves pull back with a sad sigh,

Leaving me alone under the wide, empty sky.

Unseen

I crave to be loved, yet love slips away,

A shadow unseen, though I beg to stay.

Known to the world, but a ghost in the crowd,

Voices rise loud, yet my name's not aloud.

I ache to be held, but arms never reach,

A wound never healed, a lesson they teach.

I scream, "Don't leave me!" in silence, alone—

A heart full of echoes, but never a home.

Weight of two Loves

I chose a heart that couldn't stay,
Blinded by a dream that slipped away.
Left a heart that beat my name,
Now both are ash, yet she bears the flame.

Her tears carve rivers I can't cross,
I chased a mirage, embraced the loss.
Regret's a thorn where her roses grew,
A barren field where love once flew.

The maze unfolds, a twisted game,
Her love a whisper, now just a name.
I built this prison, brick by brick,
And sentence myself, with every tick.

Two fates entwined, then torn in two,
One clings to hope, one sees it through.
I walk this labyrinth, filled with shame,
A heart of stone, consumed by flame.

Fool's Hope

She is gold, I'm just the miner.
My pickaxe claws through endless stone.
I dig with hope, but hope's a liar,
The treasure's never mine to own.

Even if I found her glow,
She'd shine for hands that aren't my own.
I know she'll never be mine, I know…
Still, I dig through rock, alone.

No map leads to where she stays,
No luck could make her heart my home.
Yet every day, I carve the maze—
Not for gold, but just to hope.

The Moth and the Tide

She doesn't come into my dreams—
Not because she's absent,
But because the night is too small for her wings.
I stitch sleep to my eyelids anyway,
Chasing the shadow of a moth
Drawn to a flame not yet lit.

Yet once... once...
Beneath a moon cloaked in velvet hush,
She emerged. Lips like smoldering coals,
Each word a note strung from a comet's tail.
The night thickened to syrup,
Dripping with the alchemy of hunger:
Her glance, my tremor,
The sonnet of a sigh
That braided time's river into the pulse of a second.

They say black holes hoard starlight for colder fates.
I'd pawn every planet to cage her here.

Her voice a landslide, her gaze a psalm.
Mountains might erode to sand,
Yet I'd memorize the eclipse of her collarbone,
The supernovas drowned in the wine-dark of her hair.

But she is a tide, not a temple.
now tsunami, now retreat. When she dissolves,
I relearn the hieroglyphs of loss:
How shadows carve her silhouette,
How even rain avoids the cracks her footsteps etched.

Still, I orbit.
Because loving her is tracing the almost,
The not yet,
The slow bleed of dusk into a horizon
Sworn only to those who kneel,
Threading prayers into sonnets, not skies.

PART IV: THE HOLLOWING

Anatomy of a Silence

A Devotion to Sadness

Dear Sadness, grant me time to bleed,
then let my bones soak tears you need.
Dear Depression, pause—let me feast,
soon you'll devour me, bite by beast.

Dear Anxiety, lend me thread—
I'll stitch a mask, then wear my stead.
Even my mind craves silent waves,
to surf the gloom where it behaves.

Dear Darkness, drown me in your tide,
and when I sink, hold nothing back.
In this abyss, I'll make my bed—

A Valut for Sorrows

I am the hollow where whispers collect,
A vault for sorrows the world won't confess.
Echoes of strangers bloom in my chest—
I hold their storms, yet no one holds mine next.

I am the dam where their currents are stored,
Their floods I contain, yet my cracks go ignored.
But when my sky cracks with thunderous weight,
I hum alone, no hands to translate.

I am the canvas for their painted woes,
A gallery of grief that no one knows.
But when I dare to sketch my own,
The brushes vanish, I'm left alone.

They say, "Speak your truth—we'll carry the sound,"
But my words dissolve where no ears are found.
Still, I open my palms, though empty they stay—
A lighthouse dimmed, guiding ships far away.

Yet here in the quiet,

I learn to be Both the wound and the whispered mercy.

For even unheld, my heart has a name:

A stone that burns, yet feels no flame.

Caged Bird

My heart is a caged bird with a thorn in its chest,
Each beat a soft whisper of her name.
It hums an old tune that the moon knows by heart,
A sad, glowing song filled with flame.

Autumn arrives, wearing colors that fade,
Yet the ache never scabs, never heals.
Leaves drop like lost moments, ruby and gold,
But the thorn stays buried, unseen.

The tune hangs in silence when daylight grows thin,
A shadow that dances till dawn.
It writes her lost name in the heart of each star,
A map made of longing, still drawn.

So the bird sings, trembling, though its feathers grow
weak, Holding love that outlasts every storm.
For even in sorrow, one truth stays alive:
Some souls are the reason we burn.

Prisoner of Night

Deep within the fluid night of my heart's voyage,

I am the ship, navigating through shadows.

You are the lighthouse I can never touch,

A beacon of light and a source of despair.

Mirage of Love

In barren lands, my spirit did roam,
Yearning for love, so far from home.
Then a vision appeared, so shimmering bright,
An oasis of hope, in soft, glowing light.

My heart filled with joy, a hopeful new start,
A promise of comfort to heal my heart.
I reached for the vision, with eager desire,
But it faded away, like a dying fire.

The desert returned, with its lonely air,
Dreams turned to dust, lost in despair.
The mirage had vanished, cruel and empty jest,
Leaving me longing, with no place of rest.

Love, Hate and the Soul

In hearts, love starts to bloom,

Hate's thorns fade, lose their room.

Joy and doubts in the mind play,

Peace in the soul lights the way.

Love's growth, with care, stands tall,

Hate's shadows shrink, they fall.

Mind's paths twist with joy and sorrow,

Soul's light brings hope for tomorrow.

Love spreads, warm and bright,

Hate's shadows vanish from sight

Why, Fate?

If destiny's real, and she's meant for other,

Why make me love her, then set her free?

Why feel this pull, so deep and so strong,

Then take her away before knowing her long?

Not one word spoken, not one shared day,

Just love that arrived, then faded away.

If destiny's real, with its grand design,

Why do so many loves fail to shine?

Why start a story, full of hope's glow,

Just to blow out the flame before it can grow?

Why let the spark catch, then drown it in rain,

Leaving only the memory of might-have-been pain?

If destiny's real, and controls who departs,

Why tear beloved ones right from our hearts?

Why build a bond, make it precious and dear,

Then vanish the one we hold ever so near?

Leaving a silence, so heavy and vast,

A future shaped by a love that couldn't last?

Why, God? The sky gives no reply.

If fate picks the one with whom life goes by,

Why must the partner, hand finally found,

Feel like the second love on sacred ground?

Not the first love, fierce, wild, and new,

But the one who stays when the first dream withdrew...

Why must my heart, though learning to cope,

Accept she wasn't my first, desperate hope?

And why this suffering? This constant, dull ache?

The one true companion that never will break?

When love walks out or simply expires,

Why feed these regrets, these unquenchable fires?

Why leave the thorn where the rose used to bloom?

Why make the deepest love lead straight to gloom?

Why, Destiny? This cost is too high.

Why let true closeness wither and die?

Why build the shrine, then walk away.

The Twin Shores of Absence

I stand upon a fractured isle, a man adrift and torn,
Where two vast, empty oceans of longing are born.
Not one, but two abysses yawn beneath my feet,
A bitter harvest sown where shattered heartbeats meet.

First Shore: The Beloved Moon

She is the distant silver, a moon I cannot hold,
A dream etched on the starlight, a story left untold.
I loved her with the fury of a tempest-tossed sea,
Loved her to death, offered my entirety.
Her smile, a phantom sunrise I chased through endless night,
Her voice, the siren's whisper that promised pure delight.
But she remained an echo, a shore I could not reach,
Her love, a fragile promise, forever out of speech.
I poured my soul's deep river into her silent sand,
And watched it vanish soundless, held by no command
My love: a burning pyre, consuming all within,
Her love: a cool reflection, where my fire couldn't win.

She is the unattained, the ever-fading gleam,

The author of my longing, the substance of my dream–

A dream that leaves me hollow, a vessel cracked and dry,

Beneath a sky of questions: "Why, beloved moon, why?"

Second Shore: The Unwanted Sun

She is the constant daylight, warm, insistent, near,

A love that beats upon me, radiating crystal-clear.

She loves me to death, they say, a fierce, unwavering blaze,

Her gaze a constant anchor through my desolate haze.

Her hands reach out with kindness, her tears for me are shed,

She offers sanctuary, a future to be wed.

But in her bright, strong light, I find no solace, none,

Her very devotion signals what cannot be done.

Her love, a heavy cloak, a chain I cannot bear,

A mirror showing clearly the emptiness inside me.

I see the pain 'I' cause reflected in her eyes,

A wound I cannot suture beneath these aching skies.

Her love: a deep, clear fountain, pure and undenied,

My lack: a chilling desert, where affection died.

She is the blame, the shame I can't escape,

The proof that getting love brings no peace.

Her presence screams the question: "Why can you not see?

The heart offered so freely, why won't you cherish me?"

The pain in the middle:

This is the cruelest crucible, the soul stretched on the rack,

To crave the unattainable, yet turn the loving back.

To burn for one who's distant, yet freeze before the near,

To live two kinds of dying, paralyzed by fear.

No peace resides within me, only the frantic hum

Of "madness," mind's unraveling, a mad, discordant drum.

I cannot rest, nor settle, nor find a place to stand,

Belonging nowhere truly, in water or on land.

The "what ifs" claw like vultures, the "if onlys" pierce deep,

While unspoken promises make my guilty mind cry.

Is this love's final punishment? This perfect, double failure?

To pay for wanting wildly with this disability?

To be the arrow flying and the target struck?

The hand that withholds kindness, crushed by fate's ill luck?

My chest splits down the middle, each half a separate ache,

One mourning love departed, one trembling for her sake.

I drown in silent screaming, beneath a starless dome,

A ghost within my own life, forever far from home.

The only constant rhythm? The suffering, pure and stark,

A slow erosion grinding my essence into dark.

For peace is but a phantom; my truth is to endure

This purgatory fashioned by love both impure

And pure beyond all measure, yet fatally misplaced,

Leaving only the echo: What good is this suffering?

Who chains the heart so cruelly? What a strange and unfair twist of fate dictate

The deepest wounds are fashioned by loves like storm-tossed seas?

I love, am loved, yet starve here,

on this barren, lonely span,

Neither lover nor beloved...

just a suffering, shattered man.

The Bloom of Grace

Loneliness held me softly, a shadow in the dusk,

I wandered streets the sun had left, painted in fading rust.

The world turned dim and distant—

no sound, no warmth, no light—

My heart grew numb, wrapped tightly in dreams I spun at night.

I dreamed of brighter mornings, where time could not intrude,

I dreamed of roles I thought I'd never hold:

A lover's touch, a father's proud embrace,

A child's laugh, a warrior, fierce and bold—

But dreams dissolved like fog they left no trace.

A world I built from wishes to hide my solitude.

Then—something cool and sudden.

A raindrop kissed my forehead and pulled me back again.

The sky began to tremble, each drop a whispered song,

A rhythm soft but certain, reminding me where I belong.

The pavement turned to mirrors, the air sang sweet and clear,

And every drop that found me washed away my fear.

I stood there—soaked, yet lighter—my heart began to bloom,

As rain rinsed off the dust of days and filled the cracks with bloom.

For nature knows our hidden pain, the storms we hold inside,

And sends the rain to heal us when we've lost the will to cry.

That night, the sky reminded me, through every drop's embrace—

Even the darkest loneliness can bloom with grace.

PART V: THE ECHO

Mapping the Ruins for Light

Eyelids Sigh

My eyelids sigh: "Enough now—
let the day's frayed light
and its quiet sorrows
fall away like petals.

Your heart, heavy as granite,
has held enough storms.
Let the dark cradle you—
softly, without recall."

So I let night bloom
where the world once burned,
and the weight in my chest
turned to wings.

Summer's Strom

On hot summer days,
nights hum with the horror of silence—
today, that silence melts into rain.

I, a bird, aching to sleep in this storm's roar,
I wouldn't fear drowning in this angry pour,
but my babies shiver under my drenched wings.

I wouldn't mind this downpour—
but the old man, who begs just to live,
sleeps under a tree's thin shade.

Is he soaked now, shaking with cold,
hunger gnawing his bones,
while the sky weeps what he once prayed for?
"Water, at last—but at what cost?"

I wouldn't fear this rain—
but the street dog, dragging a broken leg,

limps through streets turned to rivers,

searching for a shelter that doesn't exist.

I wouldn't cry—

but the stray kitten, who thirsted for days,

drinks from a puddle's bitter gift,

her tiny tongue lapping what no one gave.

I say to myself, "Don't worry—God tends to us all."

Yet my heart screams: "Does He see them?"

Those who need Him most

Are left in the storm, unheard.

A Borrowed Pulse

I write with secrets only storms know
my hands shake, spilling untold skies,
each word a lantern I clawed from the dark
for those who starve for meaning.

But you, reading, hunt for echoes of your name.
You dig for pieces of your story in my bones,
while truths I carved get buried by my hands
lost beneath the weight of what you came to take.

No one cracks the cipher of my chaos.
Every poem I bleed becomes your borrowed pulse,
beating in a ribcage that isn't mine.
We're all alone here, shouting at glass

this poem? Just a bridge I built from dust
where you cross without seeing me
two shadows, close enough to ache,
forever strangers.

A Star in My Eyes

She is a star who forever shines in my eyes,
Her face, a full moon, bright and beautiful—
Bathed in her light, my tender heart melts.
Her smile, a crescent moon, adorns the night,

Guiding its beauty through the deepest dark.
Clouds—others—try to veil her radiant glow,
Yet her light pierces through, defiant, bold.
Though countless stars may crowd the endless sky,

None rival her; their sparks grow dim beside.
She paints each night in hues of warmth and grace,
But I, a moonless void, ache for her glow—
To flood my hollow heart with boundless love,
And mend the shadows only she can hold.

Sunset

I stand where the sea meets the sand,

waves crash and fade like hours slipping away.

In the west sun burns, as red as a bleeding hand,

and my face glows in the water's sway—

we're mirrors, both burning, both torn,

pouring red to brighten the other's world.

You light the sky, I bleed to paint the grey,

but at the end waves claim us, twin embers undone.

your fire and my flesh bleed as one.

our borders dissolve where the dark tide comes.

No dawn to whisper how we burned as one—

still aching, still red, yet utterly alone.

Windows of the Void

Our eyes are not mere windows,

but fractures in the edifice of being –

portals where the soul might gaze out.

And tears?

Not blood,

but the phantom seepage of a spirit long evacuated.

The ghostly brine of a vacancy weeping for its own absence.

I am the Nameless One.

Not a man,

but an echo chamber sculpted by longing.

I hemorrhage for her love –

a wound that pulses against the hollow where a heart should beat.

I hemorrhage for the crushing weight of dreams unrealized –

a despair so deep it becomes the very air I do not breathe.

And what fills this silence,

this cavernous void where the soul once hummed?

"Nothing."

A final, chilling saturation.

Not with light,

not with joy,

not with substance...

but with the pure,

absolute essence of "No-Thing".

I cannot weep.

Why?

The reservoir is dry.

The last luminous shard of spirit,

the final fragment that could feel the abrasion of existence enough to cry...

is gone.

Dissipated.

So, I,

this vessel named as 'Nameless',

am filled.

Overflowing, even.

With what?

With the vast,

echoing "Nothing".

Yet...

the windows remain. Each night,

they swing open upon the abyss within.

Not to see the world outside,

but to conduct a desperate reconnaissance of the internal night.

Is it hope?

Or merely the automaton of habit,

programmed by a memory of having had something to lose?

I scan the barren landscape of my core.

"Is a single,

trapped ember of soul flickering there?"

A phantom warmth?

A forgotten resonance?

Or is this ritual merely the void staring into itself,

mistaking its own infinite darkness for a place where light could be lost...

and therefore,

perhaps,

found?

The Beauty of Holy Gray

O God, You dipped the brush in Light
and painted us in dawn's first hue—
that blinding white of newborn sight,
where every hope seemed fresh and true.
Why then, Creator, did You blend
the crushing blacks that bend and break?
Why let the shadows descend until our fragile canvases shake?

We start as breath, a gasp! A spark!
Your silver promise in the air.
Then life begins its cruel, grand art:
the scarlet gash of deep despair,
the midnight blue of prayers unheard,
the purple stain of trusted lies,
the golden thread of one kind word
that like a trembling firefly flies.
Not innocence—that fragile lace
too easily by darkness torn.
Nor void—that cold, abandoned space

where shattered spirits lie forlorn.

But Gray... Ah, Gray! Your masterpiece?
The velvet sigh when storms depart?
The silver-streaked and deep release
of every broken-open heart?
Is this the cost of being real?

The charcoal smudge of loved ones gone,
the pearl of tears we learn to feel,
the dust of dreams we labored on?

You let the ebony ink spill—
dark rivers carving through the white.
Was it Your terrible, holy will
to drown us till we find Your light?
For see—this Gray is not the tomb
where joy lies buried, cold and deep!

It is the gathering of bloom
and shadow where the angels weep.

It is the ancient mountain stone
that holds both storm and sun-warmed grace,
the dove at dusk, alone, alone,
yet finding its eternal place.

This Gray—it shimmers! Can't You see?
A thousand suns in one soft shade—
the battle lost, the victory,
the gentle peace that sorrows made.
It is the quiet after rain,
the wisdom etched in every line,
the echo of enduring pain
and mercy's everlasting sign.

So question You, Eternal Flame:
Why must the breaking make us whole?
Why is the soul's most sacred name
this blended, breathing, wounded GRAY
that holds—within its vast embrace—
both ruin and redeeming grace?
Not sameness, God—but unity!

The sea and sky in harmony,

the weathered face, the child's bright eyes…

All wear this truth beneath Your skies:

Our beauty is the scar we bear.

Our strength is woven from despair.

Our glory is this holy Gray—

The price of Love

The Light's last way

Through dark.

Your final, trembling, tear

On every cheek created here.

I know

I know the rushing wind won't stop for me,
Or touch my face because I want it to.
I know the fading light of dusk I see
Won't linger just because I ask it to.

I know the flower pushing through the stone
Blooms for the sun and rain, for them alone,
Not for my hand that cleared the earth away
To help it grow and face another day.

I know the ancient tree, where shadows lie,
Won't bend its branches when my songs drift by.
Its whispered leaves speak secrets to the air,
For clouds or stars, not knowing I am there.

I know the distant, coldly burning star
Shines down on me, though it is much too far
To see my eyes that search it in the night,
Lost in the dark, a solitary light.

"Yet still I love. Here's why I think it's true:
The greatest love asks nothing in return from you.
So I give love where love won't answer me:
A quiet word to wind that rushes free,

A gentle tear for blooms that fade and die,
Deep awe for trees that stretch up to the sky,
A silent wish sent to the distant star –
Though it won't know how wonderful you are.

This is the bittersweet, the special cost –
To love the world knowing that love is lost
The moment that it leaves your heart behind.
To find that giving love itself is kind.

The purest love expects no answer, bright,
It shines its strongest in the lonely night.
less human here, more ghost instead.

Epilogue: The Museum of Almosts

A collection of prose-style poems and reflections, capturing fleeting moments of a silent love.

Add-On Chapter: Ephemeral Thoughts

- *Her mysterious demeanor, a mirror to the ocean, draws me in. I crave to understand her, but fear the depths; the risk of drowning keeps me tethered to the shore.*

- *A silent soul, its secrets woven in poems.*

- *In a world of ordinary, you're the extraordinary butterfly, enchanting the garden of my soul.*

- *In a crowd of countless faces, yours is the only one I see.*

- *Perhaps my heart finds beauty in the distant, like the moon, the sky, and you. A longing to possess, knowing it's a wish beyond reach.*

- *It's strange, isn't it? My heart feels heavy when we're apart, but my soul feels free when you simply look at me, even from a distance.*

- *When I first saw you, your eyes ignited a spark within me. It was a raw, innocent love, like a hatchling turtle drawn to the vast ocean, unaware of its depths and currents.*

• *Her lips, like crimson rose petals, have an undeniable power. They draw me in, igniting a desire I cannot ignore, captivating my every sense. I wish to be the only one to cherish them.*

• *Each day, my heart grows heavier with love for you. This silent love will one day burst forth like an explosion, scattering beautiful secrets.*

• *It's a painful truth that my love for you remains unreturned.*

• *Blessed am I, to find love in the unloved.*

• *With her, even the seasons change in mere seconds.*

• *In the calmness of unspoken feelings, a music of emotions plays unseen.*

• *A single glance from you sets my heart ablaze, sparking a tempestuous battle between reason and desire.*

• *Her image, like a fever dream, consumes my thoughts and senses.*

- *My soul yearned for her affection, but burned with desire.*

- *My heart aches with longing for her, a wound that will not heal.*

- *I've imagined her so much that her image in my dreams now makes me nervous.*

- *Her eyes, an endless ocean, pull me in. Deeper I dive, lost in love's sweet sin.*

- *My love for you is like a steadfast oak, weathering every season, its roots eternally grounded in the depths of my heart.*

- *Like the changing seasons, my love for you evolves, but its core remains constant and unwavering.*

- *My heart unfurls like a lotus, bathed in the moonlight of your gaze. Whenever I see you, my face blossoms like a water lily under the moon's illumination. A love dreamt, a love unclaimed.*

- *Like the world, you've wrapped beauty around you, making you my entire universe.*

- *Your beauty illuminates the world around you. In your light, I find my own universe.*

- *You are my home, the one my love always seeks to reach.*

- *I'm a bee, gathering your love's sweet nectar, storing it in my heart's honeycomb. Yet, it forever remains yours to claim.*

Acknowledgements

This book, though born in solitude, was nurtured by many.

My deepest gratitude to my dear friends. Your presence is a steady rhythm in the soundtrack of my life. Thank you for the laughter, the conversations, and the light you bring, which often illuminated my path even when I wandered in the shadows of my own thoughts.

To the quiet moments and the unanswered yearnings—thank you for being my most profound teachers. You taught me that the deepest emotions often speak in a whisper.

To the **readers** who now hold these pages: thank you for giving these silent words a voice. By seeing your own story in mine, you have completed the circle of this art. This book was written for you, long before I knew your name.

Finally, to **silence** itself—my most constant companion. Thank you for the space to feel, the quiet to listen, and the courage to finally speak.

With gratitude,
Ramcharan

www.ingramcontent.com/pod-product-compliance
Lightning Source LLC
Chambersburg PA
CBHW050022170726
48282CB00025B/505
* 9 7 8 9 3 3 4 3 9 8 2 9 8 *